Thanksgiving

by Meredith Dash

ABDO
NATIONAL HOLIDAYS
Kids

www.abdopublishing.com

Published by Abdo Kids, a division of ABDO, PO Box 398166, Minneapolis, Minnesota 55439.

Copyright © 2015 by Abdo Consulting Group, Inc. International copyrights reserved in all countries. No part of this book may be reproduced in any form without written permission from the publisher.

Printed in the United States of America, North Mankato, Minnesota.

052014

092014

THIS BOOK CONTAINS RECYCLED MATERIALS

Photo Credits: AP Images, Glow Images, iStock, Minden Pictures, Thinkstock

Production Contributors: Teddy Borth, Jennie Forsberg, Grace Hansen

Design Contributors: Candice Keimig, Laura Rask, Dorothy Toth

Library of Congress Control Number: 2013952078

Cataloging-in-Publication Data

Dash, Meredith.

 Thanksgiving / Meredith Dash.

   p. cm. -- (National holidays)

ISBN 978-1-62970-047-2 (lib. bdg.)

Includes bibliographical references and index.

1. Thanksgiving Day--Juvenile literature.   I. Title.

394.2649--dc23

                    2013952078

Table of Contents

Thanksgiving

Thanksgiving is about giving thanks. Family and friends **gather** on this day.

4

Thanksgiving is every November. It is on the fourth Thursday.

6

History

The **pilgrims** were the first

to celebrate Thanksgiving.

8

9

The **pilgrims** came to North America by ship. The ship was called the **Mayflower**.

11

The first winter was hard. Many **pilgrims** did not survive. Then they met the **Native Americans**.

13

The **Native Americans** could farm, hunt, and fish. They taught the **pilgrims** to do the same.

15

The **pilgrims** were thankful for the good **harvest**. They invited their **Native American** friends to a **feast**.

17

The **pilgrims** and **Native Americans** played games. They told stories. They celebrated for three days.

18

Today's Thanksgiving

Today, many Americans

celebrate Thanksgiving.

They share a special meal.

20

More Facts

- Deer, corn, shellfish, meat, and cranberries were eaten at the first Thanksgiving.

- The **pilgrims** were English Protestants. They came to America to break away from the Church of England.

- There were 102 passengers and around 30 crew and sailors on the **Mayflower**. It took them 66 days to cross the Atlantic Ocean.

Glossary

feast – a large meal.

gather – come together.

harvest – what is gathered from ripe crops. A harvest may be vegetables, fruits, or grains.

Mayflower – the ship the Pilgrims sailed from Southampton to the New World.

Native Americans – the very first people who lived in America.

pilgrims – the people who sailed from England in 1620 and settled in Plymouth Rock, Massachusetts.

23

Index

abdokids.com

Use this code to log on to abdokids.com and access crafts, games, videos and more!

Abdo Kids Code:
NTK0472